Going Green

The Lessons Learned Series

Wondering how the most accomplished leaders from around the globe have tackled their toughest challenges? Now you can find out—with Lessons Learned. Concise and engaging, each volume in this new series offers twelve to fourteen insightful essays by top leaders in business, the public sector, and academia on the most pressing issues they've faced.

A crucial resource for today's busy executive, Lessons Learned gives you instant access to the wisdom and expertise of the world's most talented leaders.

Other Books in the series:

Leading by Example
Managing Change
Managing Your Career
Managing Conflict
Starting a Business
Hiring and Firing
Making the Sale
Executing for Results
Sparking Innovation
Making Strategy Work
Doing Business Globally

⊣⧓ LESSONS LEARNED ⧓⊢

Going Green

LES50NS
Boston, Massachusetts

Copyright 2008 Fifty Lessons Limited
All rights reserved

Printed in the United States of America
12 11 10 09   5 4 3 2 1

Library of Congress Cataloging-in-Publication Data is
available for this title.

ISBN: 978-1-4221-2643-1

In partnership with Fifty Lessons, a leading
provider of digital media content, Harvard
Business School Press is pleased to an-
nounce the launch of Lessons Learned, a
new book series that showcases the trusted
voices of the world's most experienced leaders. Through the power of personal story-
telling, each book in this series presents the
accumulated wisdom of some of the world's
best-known experts, and offers insights into
how these individuals think, approach new
challenges, and use hard-won lessons from
experience to shape their leadership phi-
losophies. Organized thematically, accord-
ing to the topics at the top of managers'
agendas—leadership, change management,
entrepreneurship, innovation, and strategy,
to name a few—each book draws from Fifty
Lessons' extensive video library of inter-
views with CEOs and other thought leaders.

A Note from the Publisher

Here, the world's leading senior executives, academics, and business thinkers speak directly and candidly about their triumphs and defeats. Taken together, these powerful stories offer the advice you'll need to take on tomorrow's challenges.

We invite you to join the conversation now. You'll find both new ways of looking at the world, and the tried-and-true advice you need to illuminate the path forward.

⊰ CONTENTS ⊱

Contents

Contents

Going Green

Articulating an Environmental Vision

Ray Anderson

Founder and Chairman, Interface

OUR COMPANY WAS twenty-one
years old, and I had never given a single
thought—not one—to what we were responsible for taking from the Earth or doing to
the Earth, the biosphere, in the making of
our products. And then we began to hear
a question, in the summer of 1994, from
some of our customers, especially interior

designers, "What's your company doing for the environment?"

We had no good answers. And when we finished double-talking, the essential answer was "nothing." Our salespeople were uncomfortable with this because they were getting questions they didn't know how to deal with. So a group in our company said that we really ought to bring people from our business around the world—by this time, our place was a global company, doing business in some one hundred countries—to assess what we were doing for the environment, begin to get some answers for these people who were asking.

They came to me with the idea of creating a new task force. I said, "Great. Go for it. And they said, "We want to bring this task force together. We want you to launch this task force with a kickoff speech [and we want you to] give this task force your environmental vision."

I didn't have an environmental vision. I did not want to make that speech to that group. I dragged my feet. But they stayed on my case. Finally, I said, "OK," and then I started to sweat what to say. The date was approaching—August 31, 1994—and I didn't have a clue what to say. But somehow I knew that "comply" was not a vision.

So I'm sweating. And a book lands on my desk. I began to thumb it, and then I began to read it. Very quickly, it becomes an emotional, epiphanal experience, a spear in the chest. The book was Paul Hawken's *The Ecology of Commerce*, and the essential message of that book is threefold: the biosphere, the living systems, the life-support systems of Earth are in decline. The biggest culprit in the decline is the industrial system, the linear take-make-waste industrial system of which my company, now twenty-one years old, is an integral part. And three, the only institution on Earth that's large enough, wealthy enough, pervasive enough, and influential enough to really lead human-kind out of the mess it's making for itself is the same one doing the greatest damage: the institution of business and industry, my institution.

Going Green

I took that message very much to heart;
I read that book and wept. And I made that
speech to that little group and launched
this new task force, with the vision to lead
our company to sustainability and beyond,
to become a restorative company, putting
back more than we take, and to do good for
Earth, not just no harm.

Soon after, we launched into a series of
acquisitions, acquiring a number of dealer
contractors to create a downstream distribu-
tion system, and then we brought all of these
new people together for their first meeting.
Now here are twenty-nine entrepreneurial
proprietors with our staffs, and I'm going to
speak to them, as I've spoken to every other
Interface group I could possibly assemble in
one room, about our new mission, this environmental commitment that we're making
to environmental stewardship to become
sustainable and even restorative.

Before I got up to speak, I heard the
whisper going around this audience that
was not familiar with Interface, "Has he
gone 'round the bend? Is he nuts?" I got
up to speak, and I confronted the question

head-on. I said, "I understand you're asking whether I have gone 'round the bend. Well, I want to tell you, yes, I have. I've gone 'round the bend because that's where our future is; that's my job. And I want to remind you that I went 'round the bend once before, twenty-one years ago, and found carpet tiles. And we've made a pretty good business out of carpet tiles. But I want you to understand, that was the warm-up. This is the main event. This is our reason for being from here forward. This is our purpose, our ultimate purpose." And that's the vision that I held up.

The lesson I learned from that is, a bold vision has to really be articulated over and over and over again; consistently, persistently, year after year after year. And when the whispers come—"Has he gone 'round the bend?"—completely either ignore them or confront them, but don't run from them.

We brought that group of people on board, one mind at a time, one person at a time, just as the entire Interface organization has come aboard one person at a time, one mind at a time. Today we have a company that is infused with enthusiasm for this mission that we're on. This higher purpose, they're embracing it.

Abraham Maslow said it a long time ago. At the very top of the hierarchy of human needs is the need for self-actualization, which translates into a higher purpose for oneself. And a shared higher purpose—you cannot beat it.

TAKEAWAYS

- ⚜ When the question "What's your company doing for the environment?" is posed, too often companies have no good answers.

- ⚜ To develop an environmental vision, organizations must recognize that the only institution capable of restoring damage is the same institution doing the greatest damage: business and industry.

- ⚐ After developing a vision, be bold and articulate that vision repeatedly, consistently, and with enthusiasm. Start with one person at a time.

Profits and Principles

Dame Anita Roddick

Founder, The Body Shop International

THE CYNICISM IN this country (the United Kingdom) is unparalleled, and it takes on a strange cover. And the cover is insight: that to be cynical means you have insight. And it's lies. It's just lack of moral courage. I saw more cynicism in the financial press—the cynicism that says that you have no value unless you just talk finances, that economic values are the only values in this world.

Going Green

I remember a case in point when we opened a soap factory in Glasgow in a place called Easterhouse, which was arguably then—fifteen years ago—the worst housing area in Western Europe. We wanted to build our soap factory there. We wanted to make it a shining example of really progressive factories: the best pay in the area, the best working conditions, the best health and security and education—everything. We also wanted to put 25 percent of the profits back into the community. Well, we did. And I thought, "We're on the side of the angels now."

The financial media really took objection to this and said we were stealing money from our shareholders' investment. There's nothing in law that says you have to maximize your profit; there's nothing at all that says that. And I thought, "This isn't about making a company brilliant or brave or exciting and learning from the Quakers; this was about just being obsessed with one group of people who were investing in you financially—could be £10, could be £100— but they have more strength than the people who've worked fifteen or twenty years with you." I remember my retort to the media was, "Up your bum. This is the way we're doing this; this is the way our company's being run."

Whether setting up an adventure playground or a drop-in center for the elderly, we chose to put our money back into the community. But it was a fight; it was a fight all the time with the media. I think it is the terrorism of the *or*. You have to either be one thing, or you have to be another. I think it's the genius of the *and*. I think you can do both. The Quakers did it: brilliantly successful, financially resolute, never lied—can you imagine that in business now?—never cheated, never stole, gave money to the community, built towns and communities, and cared for their people whom they employed.

It's a very interesting methodology, and John F. Kennedy said it brilliantly. He said, "The great enemy of the truth is very often not the lie—deliberate, contrived, and dishonest—but the myth—persistent, persuasive, and unrealistic." This notion that you can't be socially responsible and profitable isn't true; you can. You're more frugal, you don't waste, you're more environmentally aware, you're more transparent, you're more diligent, and you don't waste money. So I think that's the lie.

TAKEAWAYS

- ⚔ Cynicism in the financial press says that economic values are the only values that matter.

- ⚔ Companies can and should do good for their communities. Maximizing profit is not a legal requirement.

- ⚔ Despite the opinions of others, organizations can be both socially responsible *and* profitable; it's not a matter of *or*.

———•••———

Walk the Talk

———•••———

Vicky Pryce

*Chief Economic Adviser, Director General,
Economics, Department for Business, Enterprise, and
Regulatory Reform*

IN THE LATE 1990s, I became convinced that the next strategic issues to hit companies would be corporate social responsibility and ethics, something that was just developing as a concept.

I thought quite hard about what to do, and it was quite clear to me that I needed to set up something outside KPMG. I needed to focus in a slightly different way

Going Green

on consultancy practices and what they were beginning to do in that area. I thought about what companies should be doing generally and whether there could be a code of conduct for companies to accept—one can go around and verify afterward that the companies really follow it.

Along with a couple of colleagues, I came up with this concept of starting a company called GoodCorporation. Together with the Institute of Business Ethics, we developed a code of conduct to sell to the companies to get the brand of GoodCorporation known as a sign of good corporate behavior. If I was going to do this, I clearly needed to raise some cash, but I wasn't quite sure from where.

Soon after we decided to go ahead and develop it, I was visited by a friend from the States who had made loads of money in gas in Texas. I knew vaguely that he was moving into a new area, but I wasn't quite sure what.

I hadn't seen him for ages, and he turned up at the house for lunch. He turned up before me, so I arrived with my bags of shopping. I remember this so clearly: I started putting everything away and tidying up the plastic bags in the drawers in the kitchen table.

He said, "What are you doing?"

I said, "I'm recycling these bags. It's awful if you just throw them away because they take forever to degrade, so I use them again and again. It's a bit silly to take new bags each time you go shopping."

He said, "Really? How very interesting. Did you know I'm moving into the environmental area, and I'm now a really big player in wind farms?"

I said, "That's interesting, because I'm moving into this area of corporate social responsibility myself. I'm just in the process of raising money."

I got funding there and then. He opened his checkbook, more or less, and the business basically started off the back of that.

The lesson is that if you really want an investor to be interested in what you are doing—and clearly he knew me, in any case, and knew what I had done until then—you have to walk the talk. You have to show investors that you're committed to what you're doing and that you're really passionate about it. It's not just something that you are developing because you want to make some extra money, but it is something you really believe in.

———

TAKEAWAYS

———

- ⚔ Corporate social responsibility and ethics started becoming more important for organizations in the late 1990s.

- ⚔ One idea for holding organizations responsible came from developing a code of conduct, but to develop the code and accountability methods, funding was needed.

Walk the Talk

If you believe in what you're doing and "walk the talk," investors will recognize your commitment and be more willing to fund new ventures.

Defining Problems Correctly

Sir David Varney

*Former Executive Chairman,
HM Revenue and Customs*

I WAS A managing director of Shell U.K. and was part of the board that made the decision to dump Brent Spar in the North Atlantic [in 1995]. The decision was a technical one, made on a combination of safety and environmental grounds. Although the issue of the environment and imagery of the dumping came up, it was not regarded as the most significant; the most significant was the scientific and technical work.

Going Green

Various consultations were supposed to have taken place with U.K. and Continental governments, and we made the decision to dump.

I thought we'd made the right decision technically. I'm a scientist; I was brought up on the science side, so I thought we'd reached a sensible decision. It troubled me that we were like a community of monks talking to ourselves in a language that only we understood. I thought that was somewhat unhealthy, but I didn't have any more misgivings than that.

As the campaign became more violent in Germany, as more people in Shell started to put distance between themselves and the decision, and as the BBC carried uncritical footage provided by Greenpeace, I began to realize that we were going to have a hell of a struggle to sustain a position that, in the total picture of Shell, was not that significant.

I watched as that decision ran into more opposition. Finally, on the evening before the decision was made not to dump,

Defining Problems Correctly

I was asked to manage the retreat. I spent the next three weeks leading a handpicked team of people inside Shell to pick our way through how to get out of the mess we'd got ourselves into.

There was tremendous work done to make sure that the retreat didn't turn into a rout; that we explained the process by which we were going to consider options; that we got the Spar into a safe haven in Norway, where we considered the options. There was exhaustion. There was deep disappointment from the technical side of the house because they felt that what had been straightforward business and technical decisions were now being turned into political decisions that probably, in the end, would have unintended consequences that couldn't be seen that were worse for the environment than the decision to dump.

There was a split between those who felt that we had been wronged and had made the right decision, and another group—of which I think I was probably one of the more prominent—that felt we'd made the

wrong decision. We'd failed the exam, and
we had to go back to basics and rethink
our whole approach to decision making in
these areas where it gets very controversial
and where there probably isn't a right or
wrong answer. But we clearly brought a
quality of enthusiasm for technical answers
that was not widely shared.

There was a hearts-and-minds problem,
which we underestimated. We thought that
if a small group of technically able people
reached a conclusion, that should be good
enough. But we couldn't carry the great
mass of people in the organization, we
couldn't carry others overseas, and we had
no sensible argument to counter their view
that this was like throwing a Coca-Cola can
in a local pond. Our explanation that it was
like dumping a needle in Loch Ness didn't
quite capture the hearts and minds of the
public who were affected.

Attitudes had changed. If you're a big and
powerful company, you have a much greater
responsibility to explain what you're up to
and to do it through the perspective of many

different audiences. We have to become much more savvy about how we explain decisions, and we will now probably take different decisions because we take different factors into account.

The lesson is, when you are defining a problem, have you defined it correctly? Ask "Is the problem I'm being presented with a technical problem, or is it broader? If it's broader, are there other factors that ought to be considered?"

TAKEAWAYS

- ⊰ Even when solutions are well thought out and technically sound, sometimes hearts and minds conflict.

- ⊰ Powerful global companies have a greater responsibility to explain what they're doing, and they must do it through the perspectives of different audiences.

🪶 When faced with the challenge of how to define a problem, start by defining it correctly. The answer is frequently a result of myriad factors.

The Role of Business in Environmental Leadership

Peter Seligmann

*Cofounder, Chairman, and CEO,
Conservation International*

ONE OF THE weaknesses of the environmental movement is that it's always speaking to itself. And when you speak to yourself, you can pat yourself on the back because you believe the right things. But you're not expanding the reach. A real challenge in environmental leadership is, how do you include others? How do you get outside of the circle of friends?

When you look at the people who have to be reached if you want to create a global conservation ethic, it can't be the environmentalists. We have really spent some time thinking, how do you include everybody? How do you make the environmental tent so big that everybody is in it? They might not be called environmentalists, but they share your goals and your agenda.

About five years ago I got a phone call from a friend of mine, a man by the name of Jim Wolfensohn who at that time was the president of the World Bank. He said that he had just had a conversation with Rob Walton. And Rob Walton was and still is the chairman of Wal-Mart. He said that Mr. Walton was very interested in the environment, personally interested. And Wolfensohn said, "I've suggested he speak to you, Peter."

The Role of Business

I did get a call from Rob Walton, and we began to talk about his love of flying and nature. So I said, "Why don't you come over next week? We're going to have a planning meeting, and you can see the way we look at issues."

Rob Walton showed up, spent a couple of days. And then we agreed to go traveling. We went around to different places over the course of the next year, diving and exploring and basically teaching Rob about environmental issues. One day I said, "Rob, all your work with us is really dealing with your personal, private belief system. If we really want to change the world, we have to turn on Wal-Mart."

And Rob said, "I'm the chairman, but this is a company that is managed by the chief executive. That's a decision he's going to have to make. Lee Scott's going to have to make that decision." So I said, "Let's go talk to Lee Scott." Rob agreed, and he set up the meeting.

We went down to Bentonville, and we spent a day with Lee Scott, talking about the environment and talking about the impact of Wal-Mart. And Wal-Mart's impact is significant. It's significant because Wal-Mart has sixty thousand companies that supply them with their goods. They have 1.8 million employees. They have 180 million customers every week.

What was fascinating about that conversation is that the chief executive of the biggest corporation in the world had just had a granddaughter, is a really good person, and thought, "I don't want to have that impact on the world that's negative. What can we do?"

So we began to discuss a process of how to engage the company. What's their strategy? What's the culture of Wal-Mart for engaging the leadership of Wal-Mart? How does Lee Scott talk to his senior people? And he said, "This is how we do it."

So we brought down some people and began a process of engaging the senior people at Wal-Mart in this conversation about the power to do the right thing. Of course, the question that was asked was how to make certain they still have a profit.

The Role of Business

We began to look at some of the cost impacts of waste. They spend $300 million a year getting rid of their waste. So multiply that by ten. Over a decade that's $3 billion. What would happen if Wal-Mart turned around and said to their suppliers, "We're only going to take your supplies if you send them to us in recycled material, and the suppliers that actually do that, we're going to make you our preferred suppliers"? What you've just done is created an environment in the business world that is trying to come up with the innovations of how we do things in a right way.

But what was so fascinating was that within that corporate body of employees, the people who managed and bought and purchased goods—young people—were so excited that they could do something right and good that the people who were left out of the environmental discussion wanted in.

So in the beginning, when we began to talk about it and the conversation was, "Let's do a few low-hanging fruit just to demonstrate that this makes sense," it became a wildfire. It became a wildfire, and then everybody in the company wanted to participate. The result of including Wal-Mart in this conversation is so much greater than the effort that any individual NGO [non-governmental organization] could do.

There is a lesson here that is really important. And the lesson is that if you just look at the world through your lens and try to accomplish things on your own, you get a lot less done than if you open up and you really inspire and engage others. What I've seen from Wal-Mart is that they've added so much to the environmental movement in terms of how you really link sustainability with business. Because that's their life.

The result, in terms of the environmental leadership, in terms of the environmental movement, is massive. I can't begin to quantify it. I don't even understand it yet. I just know that, from CDs being manufactured out of cornstarch to mining companies being told, "We'll sell your minerals, your gold, and your jewelry if we can hold you accountable for how you mine," these are the reaches that we're having now. And that's because of the conversation with people who are not in the environmental movement but are outside of the environmental movement.

TAKEAWAYS

- ✦ To succeed in environmental leadership, you must reach others, not just the environmentalists.

- ✦ Start with those who have a personal interest in the environment, and then get them to engage their companies.

- ✦ When you truly inspire and engage others, you have a greater impact than when you try to accomplish things on your own.

Having the Courage to Challenge Your Business and Stakeholders

Tod Arbogast

Director of Sustainable Business, Dell

As I was interviewing for my role at Dell, I had the opportunity to interview with Michael Dell and a number of other executives. I felt the interview was going well. Michael and I were engaging in constructive dialogue. It was going well enough that I asked Michael what he expected of me in this role.

I remember; it was very profound. Michael simply said, "Courage." I remember pausing for a moment and then listening intently as Michael indicated one of the most critical success components in my role. It would be demonstrating the courage to bring challenging and difficult issues to the table for a constructive dialogue inside Dell as a business, but also to have the courage to engage in those constructive and sometimes challenging dialogues with external stakeholders.

In 2004 we were engaged by a broad set of stakeholders focused on forestry, led by ForestEthics and Todd Paglia. I was thinking, "Forestry—how does that correlate as a relative impact to Dell? Where's the prioritization of the issue of forestry degradation and forestry preservation in areas like the

boreal forest? How does that tie and correlate as a relative business impact to Dell?"
We realized we are a major cataloger. We
distribute a lot of mail, which obviously
consumes fiber resources, paper resources,
and has an impact on forestry.

During that early engagement we had
an opportunity to collaborate with Forest-
Ethics and others to build what was at the
time, and still is in our industry, the only
forestry stewardship policy that is a compre-
hensive view of our paper policies and how
Dell integrates those paper policies into
our procurement practices. We worked with
ForestEthics to build a robust set of guidelines around forestry that included a focus
on ensuring that we're not harvesting from
endangered forests, ensuring that we're
building Forestry Stewardship Council
certification into our virgin-fiber procurement. We worked on ensuring that we're
building postconsumer recycled content
into our catalogs. We set very specific targets
and objectives in each of those three criteria

that we can measure our progress against over the years.

Fortunately, we had an engaged business leader who embraced forestry in his procurement practices. Fast-forwarding from 2004 to where we are today, on average 50 percent of a catalog you'll get anywhere in the world has postconsumer recycled content embedded.

The first lesson is to always engage, to learn to dig deep in that engagement to determine if there is a mutual benefit and one that might not, at the onset, be visible. The second is, once you've found that there is a potential opportunity for mutual benefit, have the courage to bring forward an issue that may be somewhat misunderstood or challenging to your business. Have the courage to bring that issue forward and engage the business leadership on implementing change based on the mutual benefit that you've uncovered.

———•••———

TAKEAWAYS

———•••———

- Senior leaders must demonstrate courage to bring challenging and difficult issues to the table for both internal and external dialogues.

- To do this, you must engage. Dig deep to determine any mutual benefits, even those that remain unseen at first.

- After identifying opportunities for mutual benefit, bring forward issues that may be misunderstood or challenging and work toward bringing about change.

Find Compelling Ways to Explain Energy Consumption

Christina Page

Director of Climate and Energy Strategy, Yahoo!

ONE OF THE most compelling things that has happened since I got to Yahoo! in terms of managing the climate program is something that was actually simple and

Going Green

straightforward. It was an idea that came out of our all-employee green team. They said [we should] install a real-time energy-monitoring device.

This graphical interface would be called the "green screen" and would be placed in the cafeteria. It would have a touch screen where people could look at it and know by just calling up the data how much electricity, at that moment, a given building on campus is consuming.

That's a really simple thing to do, but we partnered with a group called Lucid Design Group. They designed this interface. It's interactive, colorful, and translates things into unit equivalents. So if you want to know how your building compares to another building, you can measure it in kilowatt hours; or, if that's not compelling to you, you can get a unit equivalent in laptop days or compact fluorescent lightbulb days or carbon or dollars—dollars expended by Yahoo! or dollars avoided by Yahoo! in electricity consumption.

Find Compelling Ways

This seemed like a fairly simple thing to me because for the most part I get very excited about technological fixes. My background is as an environmental consultant. We're enamored of things that are complex and involve huge shifts and big pieces of equipment. What this has really done is created a tangible way of understanding energy consumption for Yahoo! employees.

We had a chance to use it very effectively one Friday, as a matter of fact. [On that Friday] there was a demand-response event. In California during the summertime, when you have days that are very hot, there's a spike in electrical use that causes a risk of brownouts because everybody has their AC cranked. Yahoo! participates in something called a demand-response program where, when we have one of these days where the temperature creeps upwards of 100 degrees, we turn down our lights and we crank down our AC system.

What that does is help our local utility to consume less energy so we're not at risk for

Going Green

a brownout. We're reducing our energy consumption, we're reducing our carbon
footprint, and we're preventing the system
from getting overloaded. Now, that's something that typically the way an employee sees
it is, "My aisle's too hot, and my cube is
underlit." And this is an inconvenience.

What we're able to do by using the
green screen is put it in the context of the
environmental implications and the larger
implications. Seeing the energy use for all
of our buildings spike and then suddenly
seeing them decrease when the demand
event was called and we reduced our
energy consumption has a remarkably
profound impact on the way that employees understand and frame a demand-
response event.

In terms of the green screen, that's a
tool that I didn't think would be nearly as
compelling as it turned out to be. People
really do like being able to measure things
and see them, and how you present them in
terms of sustainability is potentially a really
compelling message—if you can figure out

a way to make it tangible to people, if you make it graphically visible and tangible on the ground.

It's a matter of looking at, here's what your building is consuming today, in the middle of a really hot day in California. That puts things in a context people can really understand and feel inspired by to take action. People are a lot less compelled by abstract ideas about kilowatt hours than they are about things that you make as tangible and clear to understand as possible.

TAKEAWAYS

- ⚔ It's possible to create compelling environmental initiatives that are simple and straightforward.

- ⚔ Technology can play a significant and tangible role in helping people

understand the effects of such environmental programs.

✠ People like being able to measure and
see things, and providing graphically
visible information garners greater
enthusiasm.

Challenges of CSR to Management Teams

Andrew Kakabadse

Professor of International Management Development,
Cranfield University, School of Management

A LOT OF common thinking today places
CSR and the whole of corporate responsibility on the shoulders of management and
not so much the board, with the idea being

that the board is a bit removed from reality.
What we're finding from other surveys—we
now have about 12,500 organizations
spanning twenty-one countries—is that
there are two or three trends.

The first trend is, about a third of the
world's top teams are permanently divided
on vision. So you'll have the chief executive and the various directors going into
meetings, having a really good discussion,
making a clear decision, and then walking
out of the meeting and doing something
different to what they just decided. [And all
that time] many of the people, before they
go into the meeting, have decided that
they will break whatever vows they made at
the meeting.

The second trend that we're finding with
top teams is inhibition. The big problem
here is that if many of the directors feel
uncomfortable about a particular subject,
often because somebody's championed it—it
could be the chief executive and that would
be his or her baby—it's difficult to raise the
subject. What you have is people who know

what's wrong with the company, who know what to put right, and who know that the consequences of saying nothing—and will still say nothing.

What emerges from this is that about one-third of the world's organizations have worked very hard to have a dynamic top team that is clear on what it's supposed to be doing and speaks the truth. And two-thirds of the world's top teams are constantly working their way toward that [goal] and never really achieving it. The unit of analysis is the organization. Each organization has tension. That tension translates itself right from strategy to application and operations. When you're dealing with synergies that are on the softer side—on the belief side or on the people side—that tension becomes worse if there isn't a unified top team.

In many ways, you can place CSR and the reality of CSR almost like management training or some of the equality movements that are taking place in companies. In certain organizations they are firmly pushed through because you have a top team that really believes in what it's doing, but in most places, you'll get some deviation of practice (i.e., "we intended to do this, the words were nice, the words written on paper were even better"). But then the practice becomes quite difficult.

The advice to companies would be, where is the point in the structure of the organization where the tensions really begin to arise? The strategic tensions are obviously at the top, but if you've decided on a CSR strategy, [even just] to look good to the outside world, there is at least an attempt to try and push some sort of CSR innovation down the line. But the further down the line you go, there will be a difference of opinion between the CSR strategy and its application and costs.

In today's mature markets, where you make money as much by being cross-disciplinary as by making profit, which line managers are really going to spend and invest in CSR when they also have particular budget constraints to fulfill? The critical issue is, where are those tension points? Is there just one? Are there two or three?

And the managers just above the individual who is tasked with making CSR work, what are their opinions about CSR? That is a critical factor. Those individuals are sufficiently far enough from senior management to allow their opinion to form practice. So unless you see what the manager thinks, what the manager's manager thinks, and the reality of push to make sure that your costs are always clean and well disciplined, you won't really understand how to make CSR work.

Number one, identify the tension points in the structure. Number two, understand the degree to which cost and cost management are really part of the business of the organization. And number three, have an open debate about it. I suspect number three is a sensitive [issue] because if you have an open debate, you then have to bring to the top team's attention that they're not doing what they said they were doing, and that's sensitive.

TAKEAWAYS

- The successful implementation of corporate social responsibility often falls to senior management, but therein lies part of the challenge.

- Top teams are often divided on vision, teams are fearful of pointing out problems, and tensions affect strategy and operations.

- To lessen the challenges, focus on the individuals who are tasked with implementing CSR practices. Get their buy-in by learning about how CSR affects their part of the business and by engaging them in debate.

Tying Environmental, Social, and Financial Benefits Together

Jean Sweeney

Vice President, Environmental, Health and Safety Operations, 3M

WHEN WE TALK about innovation and sustainability, one of my favorite examples is Post-it products. Previously in my career

Going Green

I was the Post-it manufacturing operations
manager, and I was involved in the development of water-based adhesives for Post-it.
In the past, Post-it adhesive was developed
using a solvent-based process and is the
product that we sold in the marketplace
when we first invented the product. Over
time, though, I became very much aware
that [using] solvent as a method for production was not going to be sustainable in
the long term.

So a great deal of effort was put into
developing a water-based adhesive, which
we believed would be able to not only do
a better benefit for the environment but
also, more specifically, could reduce our
cost. This took quite a long period of time,
first with the intention of replacing the
solvent-based adhesive with the water-based
adhesive and having similar performance or
the same performance characteristics as you
have come to expect in a Post-it Note.

But over time with that R&D work, we
discovered that we could not only do similar
characteristics but actually enhance those

characteristics with performance that actually exceeded our previous, solvent-based formulation. So we had not only a cost benefit but also a performance benefit that we were able to sell and market with our products under the Super Sticky brand, which allows a consumer to be able to use a Post-it Note on a vertical surface in addition to it being used on paper. It gave consumers a much wider variety of surfaces to be able to attach the product to.

My personal involvement in that was in getting the approval for the money that would be spent to build the manufacturing equipment that would be used to produce the water-based product, because it could not be produced on the previous equipment. It required a new technology and manufacturing process, and a key part of presenting that and getting the approval for the money included the cost reduction that we knew that we would be able to achieve with this new process.

It would be an investment initially, but obviously [we were] expecting a significant rate of return on that investment over time with the production of a water-based adhesive, and that product, that financial commitment was met and certainly received by the executive board as the right direction to go in. Even though it was a large expenditure, they were very much in support of it.

We began with that process, and in 2003 the water-based Post-it Note was introduced. It has been very successful in the marketplace since then. The most important thing I learned is that we were able to tie together not only an environmental benefit and certainly a social benefit, too—because for the safety and health of employees working in that area, it was a benefit for them—but also we tied that with a financial benefit, not only to ourselves but also to our shareholders. It was a great example of tying all three of those together.

TAKEAWAYS

- Even with highly successful products, production methods may not be sustainable in the long term.

- New R&D investment can pay off in products that are better for the environment, create cost savings, and perform better.

- In the long run, it's a win-win situation for the environment, for employees, and for stakeholders.

Working in Partnership

Stephen Tindale

Former Executive Director, Greenpeace UK

PEOPLE HAVE HEARD, over the last thirty years, a lot about the environmental message, a lot about environmental problems. And it's tended to be couched in terms of the fact that you have the environmentalists on one side and you have industry on the other—and there's not much meeting of minds in the middle.

Going Green

It's much more powerful if you can say to people, say to government, and say to the public that on some issues there is a meeting of minds; both business and the environmentalists can say, "This is the way forward, this is good business and good for the planet." When you get what is seen as two sides of the argument coming together and putting forward a single message, that message is much more likely to be accepted.

Greenpeace has been campaigning in favor of renewable energy for years, but we particularly felt in the U.K. that offshore wind was an enormous potential because we have so much wind in this country, and we have a lot of sea, and we don't have that much land where we can put them onshore. So we wanted to build the country's first offshore wind farm. We wanted a company that was rich enough, committed enough, and prepared to commit to a partnership with Greenpeace to make that a reality.

So we went out with a tender document, effectively. We went out to several companies and said, "Can you deliver this?" And npower was the company that came closest to what we were asking for.

This was an unlikely partnership between Greenpeace and npower, because on the one hand you have a large energy [company] that has still quite a lot of fossil fuels in its portfolio—it's a large burner of coal, which is a very serious contributor to the greenhouse effect. On the other hand, you have a radical campaigning organization that hasn't traditionally been very friendly with business.

But that was the reason it was an effective partnership: because, first of all, we sat down and worked out that although there were things that we disagree about—we think npower should stop burning coal; they probably think that we should stop doing some of the things that we do—more importantly than that, we have a single very important, very concrete thing that we did agree on. We agreed to differ on the areas of disagreement and cooperate where we did agree—on the common purpose of building a wind farm.

I personally take three lessons from this partnership with npower. First, I was very struck when I met with the [partnership's] then–chief executive, Brian Count, that he actually knew a lot more about renewable energy than I did, because he had spent a lot of his career working on marine energy. There is sometimes a temptation among environmentalists to assume that people in industry don't think about these things. Actually, there's an immense amount of expertise out there, and we were able to tap into it, finding the right person in the right place.

The second lesson was that it's been very time-consuming. Working in partnership has been often very frustrating because they see things slightly differently, we see things slightly differently, and there's a lot of working through to iron out the differences. And at times it's felt like, "Is it really going to be worth it in the end?" It's a lot simpler to go off and do your own thing. And there has been a degree of internal resistance at times, not really because they didn't like the idea, but just people were questioning whether it was worth the commitment in terms of time.

But the third lesson, the overwhelming lesson is that for all the difficulties, for all the frustration of working in partnership, it delivered something we couldn't possibly have done on our own. Of course, we could retain our purity and not have anything to do with any of these companies that have any fossil fuels in their portfolio, but the result of that would be wind farms would not be built, or they wouldn't be built nearly as quickly.

There's an urgent climate crisis out there that people are becoming more and more aware of, and we need to tackle it. And we need to tackle it by doing what needs to be done, which means working in partnership with those who have the solutions.

TAKEAWAYS

⚞ In business you're sometimes faced with environmentalists on one side and industry on the other, with little meeting of minds in the middle.

⚞ By partnering with others, even when you have to agree to disagree on certain issues, you can send a more powerful message and are more likely to see the two sides of the argument come together.

⚞ By finding common purpose and working in partnership with those who have the solutions, you're better able to succeed at doing what needs to be done.

Developing Policies on Environmental Sustainability

Bob Wigley

Chairman, Europe, Middle East, and Africa,
Merrill Lynch & Co.

THE QUESTION IS, how do we respond
to questions from staff about the whole
issue of environmental sustainability? The

first thing to say is, we get more questions
on this subject than almost any other. It has
really caught people's imagination—people
who do think very responsibly about their
planet. It's really got people going.

The second thing I noticed is that when
I go to recruiting visits at universities, it's
also a question that we're asked very consistently: "What are your policies about
environmental sustainability?" So there's
no question the company has to have a very
developed approach to this subject. And
it's really in two areas. First, it's about having some policies; and second, it's about
having some initiatives.

So on policy, we have to decide who we
will act for and who we won't act for. For
example, if a company was going to build a
nuclear power plant in Kazakhstan, is that
something we would do or something we
would not do? Obviously, we look at every
transaction on a case-by-case basis, but we
look to see that the company concerned is
adopting an environmentally responsible
approach in the project that we might be

financing or advising on. And if we're not happy, we won't do it.

We train all our staff so that they [are doing] due diligence on the projects that we're working on. And it's a two-stage process. Number one, will we do it in the first place as a matter of policy? Then, second, once we're into the project, are we happy that the company is living up to the obligations that it has set out? That's if you like the policy.

On the initiatives, [there is] a whole different range of issues. For example, we have developed a fantastic business trading carbon credits. This is the concept of basically selling a credit to encourage people to build their plants in an environmentally sustainable way, and we're a world leader in that area, particularly in Europe. We have a number of deforestation projects. One of the quickest ways to have an impact on climate change right now is to stop deforestation. I think something like 20 percent of the issue arises per annum right now from deforestation.

So again, we've taken the carbon-credit idea, we have our own deforestation credit, and we're doing this in Indonesia right now. Basically, the funds go back to the locals who would have made money from chopping the wood and selling it, so they're still getting the money; and we're taking money from people who want to do something about deforestation. This is mixing business and philanthropy, but [also] really having a very dramatic impact on the climate change.

The third issue is around our own offices. We developed something called the "turn it off" campaign. We brought our staff in and said, "What can you do in our office in London, where we have four thousand people, to help save energy?" A whole range of initiatives—silly things—but we obviously have hundreds and hundreds of trading screens that people used to leave on every night. They now turn them off before they go home. Recycling. How we use cars to come to work or not, and encouraging people to cycle. Lots and lots of different initiatives, but all of them in their own little way contributing to, everybody's personal contribution to, climate change.

The lesson learned is, involve your people, because actually your people have the most creative ideas. You can sit there and try and develop a policy, but if you get a bunch of people in a room, if you're normally employed dreaming up business ideas, and say, "Right, let's apply that creative talent to how we save the planet," you'd be amazed what they come up with. The main lesson learned is, use your people, because they have the talent.

TAKEAWAYS

⊨ The concept of environmental sustainability has caught people's imaginations and is one that today's companies must be able to address.

Going Green

- Organizations must develop both policies and initiatives, each of which have their own set of challenges.

- Businesses must change the way their own staffs think. By involving staff, companies can tap into truly creative solutions.

Lessons from Mother Teresa

Stephen Howard

CEO, Business in the Community

FIFTEEN YEARS AGO I was given my
first major international job with the
company that I was with and put in charge
of a couple of divisions that had overseas
operations. We were expanding the business
rapidly and opening new factories all over
the world, including India. I was on my way
to the opening of a plant in Calcutta.

Going Green

I flew from New York to Bombay. I was
waiting for my plane to go on to Calcutta,
standing in line to get my connecting ticket,
when someone mentioned that Mother
Teresa was in the airport. I hadn't seen her.
I didn't even know what Mother Teresa
looked like. I didn't really think any more
of it than that. I waited in the lounge, was
called to our flight, and boarded the plane.
It was a small, crowded, hot plane, waiting
out on the tarmac.

The plane gradually filled up. Every seat
on the plane filled except the one next to
me. We're waiting and waiting and waiting,
and who gets on the plane? This is a true
story—Mother Teresa gets on the plane. She
comes down and sits next to me, and I'm
sitting at the window on this crowded plane.
She sits next to me, and she was a short little
thing with sort of a curvature of the spine,
so she was leaning over in her seat. The
plane, of course, is abuzz as Mother Teresa
gets on. Most of the people flying were
Indian and were from Calcutta or Bombay,
so there was a great deal of excitement.

Lessons from Mother Teresa

She sat next to me and introduced herself. I was quite impressed, so I introduced myself to her. She seemed slightly less impressed, I would say, but we had a very nice chat. We were probably a minute or two into the preliminaries of the conversation, the sort of top layer that one has. She asked me—or at least I thought she asked me— "What do you do?" I was about to launch into my "I'm a captain of industry" story. I was very proud of this new role I had, very excited about opening this factory in Calcutta, and feeling good about myself with my new promotion.

I began to launch into this story, and she said, "No, Stephen, what do you do that really matters?"

I thought, "Now that is a tough old question." This little voice whispered in my ear, "You can't lie to Mother Teresa." I thought, "Dear me."

We had a wonderful hour-long conversation about the roles that leaders have in tackling issues of social import in the world. It was interesting. Never once did she ask

Going Green

me to do anything for her. She didn't ask
for any money. She didn't even chastise
me for my rather weak answers. We had
a relatively probing conversation about
what my role was in the world as a business
leader. What did I think of both my faith
and my view of society and of humanity?
How did those things all come together?
I have to confess I didn't have at the time,
and I'm not sure I have now, particularly
good answers to those questions. It surely
gave me an awful lot to think about.

It was probably five months later; I was at
Washington National Airport waiting for a
taxi out in front, having just arrived from
someplace or another. Who walks out of a
car to go into the terminal but Mother Teresa again? This time she had a whole bevy
of other nuns with her. They were all about
four feet high, but there were a lot of them.
I don't know whether she remembered
me or not—probably not—but I certainly
remembered her, so I went up and talked
to her. She acted like she did, and she asked

me something along the lines of what had come from our conversation.

I look back on that time, and it was a formative moment for me. I was just at the point where the career I thought I wanted was in ascent. I had gotten the job that I had been lusting over. It was a good job, and I enjoyed it. And I hope I did a reasonable job with it. I was proud of the factory that we were opening, but I realized from that conversation with her that my view of what the success in Calcutta would look like was probably too narrow. My sense of our role as a major employer in that impoverished land—or in Illinois, for that matter—was too narrow.

It was one of those moments that really began to make me think. As I thought back over time, and as I thought about the journey that I've been on as a businessperson and in the other things that I've done in my life, I keep harkening back to that conversation. I often ask myself, "What would I say to Mother Teresa if she asked me about this situation that I'm in, what I'm doing, what my priorities are, or how I've changed?"

TAKEAWAYS

- There's a big difference between the questions "What do you do?" and "What do you do that really matters?"

- Leaders have an obligation to tackle issues that have social impact, and they accomplish that by joining their faith and their views of society and humanity.

- When our ideas of success are too narrow, it can be helpful to consider, "What would I say to Mother Teresa if she asked me about this situation or my priorities?"

Managing Sustainability Issues Takes a Systemswide Approach

Adrian Hodges

Managing Director,
International Business Leaders Forum

ONE OF THE biggest challenges I see at the moment is coming to terms with the fact that the boundaries of accountability—that is, what they're being held responsible for by different sections of society—are very much a moving feast, if you like.

I'll give you one example. I was working with a U.S.-based soft-drinks company and advising them on their management of their sustainability and their approach to different stakeholders on social issues. I remember walking into their office in the U.S. one day and then very proudly laying on the table a well-produced and glossy social report. It was their first social report, and it contained some wonderful examples of the positive things that they as a business around the world were doing for the communities where they were operating. Good news. I gave words of encouragement, and they agreed that in the future this report needed to be perhaps a bit more evidence based, with some stretch goals.

I got back to London, and that same evening on my return, the news hit the press that this same company was being accused of complicity in the murder of trade unionists within a bottling plant. Now, the company denied those allegations vehemently, but they also said that this actually was a bottler's issue, not their issue. It was a separate company and therefore had actually nothing to do with them. Now, in the world of global brands, this was a nuance too far for most consumers and most commentators, who really linked the activities and the behavior of the company together with the one brand.

The company undertook a very detailed research of the accusations and put a number of steps in place to really address the issue. But it struck me, as I was then refreshing my memory of this annual review of their social impact. As I looked through it, I could see that about half the stories in it were actually positive stories about the impacts of the bottlers—these same people whom the company had claimed were actually a separate entity from them.

You can't have it both ways, and the business soon realized that. The company is now under completely new management.

Going Green

And it's made great strides to work with its bottlers and others across the value system of the business to set standards and guidelines and indeed to support improvement in working and labor conditions through the various players in that business market. So there you have an example of extended responsibility from an external stakeholder perception and the company taking some very concise and precise action to address that. Inconsistencies through that system are not good for the business.

The lesson from this particular example is at the heart, really, of how companies manage sustainability issues and [how they] recognize that they need a systemswide approach—one that takes in the dots, joining up the dots, if you like, between the different parts of the business. Upstream and downstream. And [they must recognize] that the company needs to use its influence, and that can be soft power. Also, it can actually be hard power in terms of the contractual relationships and the standards that are set.

TAKEAWAYS

- One of the biggest challenges organizations face is coming to terms with the fact that the boundaries of accountability are very much a moving feast.

- Companies must remain accountable. It's not acceptable to both claim and disown various entities depending on the situation.

- Organizations need to implement a systemswide approach that links in the various parts of the business and exert their influence when called for.

Sustainability Needs a Business Case

Truett Tate

Group Executive Director, Lloyds TSB

A GOOD STORY that makes the connection between sustainability as a vision and sustainability in practice? Probably the best would be that I'm the chairman of Lloyds Development Capital. That's our private equity business: LDC, Lloyds Development

Going Green

Capital. They were wrestling with how sustainability fits with what they do.

In our board meetings, we talked about the possibility [of sustainability]: "Well, it probably means if we find a company that's involved in this space, we support them even if we're not so certain that the economics would warrant it." That was a principle. We all looked at one another and wrestled a bit with that. Certainly kind of ticks the box that says you're supporting the direction, but is that in itself sustainable if what you've done is support something that doesn't give you a return and you perhaps lose money? Does anyone really do it again?

So we said, "We're in the right direction, but how do we make that sustainable?" And the concept was, "All right, let's find a company that's in the space, that doesn't necessarily have a model that's over-whelmingly positive, and see what we could do to change their probability of success."

A good example early on was, we found a company that is engaged in some new technology in light switches and dimmers, helping homes and offices be more efficient in terms of their footprint. And we said, "OK, a company looks well designed, reasonably well capitalized. [But there is] some question in terms of absolute market. Why don't we invest in them and start using their products in our buildings? So we will test [the technology] in terms of its success, we'll become testimonials for it, we'll actually generate revenue for them to the degree that it works, and we can spread it in more and more buildings."

And what we found was a model that we've used with a number of companies since, which is to identify a good idea in this space and then find a way to actually use it and in using it make them successful.

In some cases they changed the product line because it wasn't necessarily what was promised. We worked with them, tested it for the second or third generation, and found out that we were able to get a great return on our equity because we helped them make a more successful company. Probably the best advice is something that's been said before, and it is a truism, which is, sustainability, there needs to be a business case.

It's not just for the contribution to the better global outcome. But the business case doesn't have to be understood in a vacuum. There's a formula, and the element that some people forget in the formula is that you can change the course of the outcome. It's not up to the proposal. It's chemistry, and one of the ingredients is your own engagement. You can be the catalyst that changes the outcome.

TAKEAWAYS

⊣ Companies must make the connection between sustainability as a vision and sustainability in practice.

Sustainability Needs a Business Case

- ⚎ When you identify a good idea, find a way to use it and make it successful.

- ⚎ Though business cases have a formula, your engagement can be the catalyst that changes the outcome.

ABOUT THE
CONTRIBUTORS

Ray Anderson is the Founder and Chairman of Interface, Inc., one of the world's largest interior furnishings companies. He is also the company's former President and CEO.

Mr. Anderson began his career in the carpeting and textile businesses while at Deering-Milliken and Callaway Mills. In 1973 he founded Interface and began producing free-lay carpet tiles in the United States. That same year he partnered with Britain's Carpets International, which he took over 20 years later.

Today Interface is still a leader in its core business, modular soft-surfaced floor coverings. Mr. Anderson is recognized as one of the world's most environmentally progressive businesspeople, and Interface is known as a leader in the green business movement.

Mr. Anderson served as Cochairman of the President's Council on Sustainable Development during the Clinton administration. He also serves on the boards of Melaver, Inc.; the Georgia Conservancy; the Ida Cason Callaway Foundation; and Rocky Mountain Institute. He is an adviser to the

About the Contributors

Center for Sustainable Development at the University of Texas at Austin.

Tod Arbogast is the Director of Sustainable Business at Dell Inc., the direct-sales computer company.

In this position Mr. Arbogast is responsible for overseeing Dell's sustainability team and programs, managing the balance of Dell's growth strategy with the goal of minimizing Dell's impact on natural and human resources.

Prior to joining Dell in 2000, Mr. Arbogast was Senior Director and part of the founding team of eMachines, Inc., a desktop and notebook PC vendor, where he managed the warranty and non-warranty support components of the company's service delivery division.

Adrian Hodges is the Managing Director at the International Business Leaders Forum, where he specializes in issues of corporate responsibility as they relate to international business strategy and practice.

He has managerial experience in business, local government, and nongovernmental organizations. He joined IBLF in 1998 and held a number of positions, including Director, the Americas, and Director, Marketing and Communications, before becoming Managing Director.

Prior to IBLF, Mr. Hodges was worldwide Head of Corporate Communications for retailer Body

Shop International Plc. Before that he was Director of Communications and Marketing for Business in the Community.

Stephen Howard is the Chief Executive Officer of Business in the Community, a consortium of organizations committed to improving their impact on society.

Mr. Howard joined BITC as Managing Director in September 2005. Before his appointment, he spent eight years as a supporter and national partner of BITC's Business Action on Homelessness initiative.

Mr. Howard began his career as a lawyer and partner with Adler Pollock & Sheehan, P.C. He was appointed General Counsel at Cookson America, Inc. in 1985.

In 1997 Mr. Howard was appointed Group CEO of the Cookson Group, Plc, culminating in his appointment as Group Chief Executive, a role he held until 2004. Between 2004 and 2005, he served as Group Chief Executive of Novar, Plc.

Andrew Kakabadse is Professor of International Management Development at Cranfield University School of Management.

Professor Kakabadse has published 30 books and over 190 articles, including "Politics of Management" and "The Wealth Creators." His current areas of interest focus on leadership, change management, improving the performance of top executives and their teams, consultancy practice, social and public administration, organizational behavior, and international relations.

He is undertaking a multinational study of boardroom effectiveness and governance practice.

Christina Page is the Director of Climate and Energy Strategy, Yahoo! Inc., the largest knowledge-sharing community on the Web.

Ms. Page began her career in 1992 as an Editorial Assistant with National Public Radio. She then served as a Field Instructor for the National Outdoor Leadership School, from 1995 to 2000.

Prior to joining Yahoo!, Ms. Page worked at Rocky Mountain Institute, a nonprofit that fosters the efficient and restorative use of natural, human, and other capital; there she served as a member of the RMI Integrative Design Team and project leader for RMI's educational initiatives starting in 2001.

Vicky Pryce is the Chief Economic Adviser and Director General, Economics, of the Department for Business, Enterprise and Regulatory Reform (formerly a component of the Department of Trade & Industry).

Ms. Pryce has held a variety of senior positions, including Corporate Economist at ESSO Europe, with responsibility for Europe, the Middle East, and Africa; and Chief Economist for KPMG, a firm she joined in 1986. During her time there she was the partner in charge of economic consultancy, strategy services, and international privatizations.

After working as a partner in the strategy and policy division of London Economics, she joined the Department of Trade and Industry (DTI) as Chief Economic Adviser and Director General, Economics. She continues in that role for the Department for Business, Enterprise and Regulatory Reform, which was created in June 2007 along with the Department of Innovation, Universities and Skills to replace the DTI.

Over the past 15 years Ms. Pryce has directed or participated in a large number of major consultancy assignments, both in the United Kingdom and internationally, for both the private and public sectors. This includes policy evaluations for U.K. government departments including the Department of Trade & Industry, the Treasury, and the former Inland Revenue.

Ms. Pryce is also Joint Head of the Government Economic Service and a member of the international advisory board of BritishAmerican Business, Inc. She is also a Fellow of the Royal Society for the Encouragement of Arts, Manufactures and Commerce (RSA) and cofounder and adviser to GoodCorporation Ltd.

Dame Anita Roddick is the founder of the Body Shop International, Plc.

Originally, she trained as a teacher. She then worked for the United Nations in Geneva before running a restaurant and hotel in Littlehampton, West Sussex.

She started the Body Shop in Brighton in 1976 to create a livelihood for herself and her two daughters while her husband was trekking across the Americas. She had no business training, but economic necessity—combined with the colorful experiences she had gained from her various travels—saw the creation of a successful business dedicated to the pursuit of social and environmental change.

The Body Shop went public in 1984. It has grown from one store in England to a multinational company with nearly 2,000 stores in 50 countries.

Anita Roddick became a Dame Commander of the British Empire in July 2003 for her services to retailing, the environment, and charity. She died in September 2007.

Peter Seligmann is the Cofounder, Chairman, and CEO of Conservation International, an organization that creates lasting solutions to biodiversity and conserves the Earth's living heritage.

Mr. Seligmann received his master's degree from the Yale School of Forestry in 1974, and soon after, he began a job in conservation. Nearly a decade later he moved overseas. During a visit to Peru, he was struck by the contrast between the country's enormous biological wealth and its staggering poverty. It was then, in 1987, that he cofounded Conservation International, based on a vision that people could live peacefully with nature. Since then the organization has grown to 45 field offices on four continents.

In 1998, Conservation International established the Center for Applied Biodiversity Science, and in 2001, the Center for Environmental Leadership in Business. In 2000, Conservation International launched the Critical Ecosystem Partnership Fund in collaboration with the World Bank and the John D. and Catherine T. MacArthur Foundation.

In 2001, Mr. Seligmann was awarded the Netherlands' Order of the Golden Ark. He serves on the board of the Wild Salmon Center in Portland, Oregon, and the advisory councils of the Jackson Hole Land Trust, Ecotrust, and other not-for-profit organizations, including Japan's Keidanren Nature Conservation Fund. In 2000, President Clinton named him a member of the Enterprise for the Americas Board.

Jean Sweeney is the Vice President, Environmental, Health and Safety Operations for 3M Company, a recognized leader in research and development.

She is a graduate of Montana State University with a BA in chemical engineering and an MBA from the University of St. Thomas. Ms. Sweeney joined 3M upon graduation from MSU and has had a diversity of assignments, including product development, manufacturing management, and general business management. She has had two international assignments: Manufacturing Director for 3M Australia in Sydney and Managing Director of 3M Taiwan in Taipei.

About the Contributors

Truett Tate is the Group Executive Director of Lloyds TSB Bank, Plc, a leading U.K.-based financial services group.

Mr. Tate joined the group in 2003 as Managing Director, Corporate Banking, before being appointed to the board in 2004. From 1972 to 1999 he served with Citigroup, where he held a number of senior and general management appointments in the United States, South America, Asia, and Europe. He was President and Chief Executive Officer of eCharge Corporation from 1999 to 2001 and Cofounder and Vice Chairman of Chase Cost Management, Inc. from 1996 to 2003.

Mr. Tate is a Director of BritishAmerican Business, Inc. and a member of the fund-raising board of the National Society for the Prevention of Cruelty to Children (a British organization).

Stephen Tindale is the former Executive Director of Greenpeace UK. He is currently a visiting research fellow at the Policy Studies Institute, a leading independent research institution in London.

Mr. Tindale started his career as a diplomat. His four years in the British Foreign and Commonwealth Office, included a year at the British Embassy in Pakistan. After that he joined Friends of the Earth, where he was the organization's air-pollution campaigner.

Following this he spent two years at the Fabian Society. He then went to work for Chris Smith, MP, who had recently been appointed Shadow Environment Secretary. After two years in this role, he moved to the Institute for Public Policy Research (IPPR), where he worked on green taxes and energy policy.

He then became the Director of Green Alliance. However, he was taken from this position after the 1997 elections to be Special Adviser to Michael Meacher when he became Environment Minister. Mr. Tindale held this position for two years before deciding he would be more effective trying to influence change from outside the system. In April 2001 he moved to Greenpeace UK as Executive Director. He left the position in 2007.

Sir David Varney is the former Executive Chairman of HM Revenue and Customs, the United Kingdom's customs and tax department.

Sir David has held a variety of senior roles within the oil organization Royal Dutch Shell, Plc, including the positions of Managing Director of AB Svenska Shell in Sweden and Director of Shell International, with responsibility for Shell's oil products business in Europe. From 1996 to 2000 he was Chief Executive Officer of BG Group, Plc (formerly British Gas Corporation), where his experience spanned both the United Kingdom and overseas markets.

In 2001 he became Chairman of mm02, a provider of mobile communications services. From September 2004 to August 2006 he was Executive Chairman of HM Revenue and Customs, the de-

partment created from the integration of HM
Customs and Excise and the Inland Revenue. Sir
David chaired Business in the Community from
2002 to 2004 and was President of the Chartered
Management Institute from 2005 to 2006.

Sir David is the former President of the council
for the Institute of Employment Studies. He also
serves as the Prime Minister's Adviser on Public
Service Transformation.

Bob Wigley is the Chairman, Europe, Middle East,
and Africa, of Merrill Lynch & Co., Inc., a leading
wealth management, capital markets, and advisory
company.

In his current role Mr. Wigley serves Merrill
Lynch's clients in the region across the businesses
and ensures that proper governance and integration
are in place.

He has held a number of management positions
at Merrill Lynch, serving as Chairman of EMEA
Corporate Banking from 2003 to 2004, global
Cohead of Telecom and Media Investment Banking
in 2002, Cohead of U.K. Investment Banking in
2001, and Cohead of Corporate Broking in 2000.
In these roles he was instrumental in closing a number of Merrill Lynch's most significant European
banking transactions and building a successful
European franchise.

Mr. Wigley joined Merrill Lynch from Morgan
Grenfell in 1996.

⊰ ACKNOWLEDGMENTS ⊱

First and foremost, a heartfelt thanks goes
to all of the executives who have candidly
shared their hard-earned experience and
battle-tested insights for the Lessons
Learned series.

Angelia Herrin at Harvard Business
School Publishing consistently offered
unwavering support, good humor, and
counsel from the inception of this ambi-
tious project.

Brian Surette, Hollis Heimbouch, and
David Goehring provided invaluable editorial direction, perspective, and encouragement. Much appreciation goes to Jennifer
Lynn for her research and diligent attention
to detail. Many thanks to the entire HBSP
team of designers, copy editors, and marketing professionals who helped bring this
series to life.

We would also like to thank Professor
David Grayson and the Doughty
Centre for Corporate Responsibility

Acknowledgments

(www.doughtycentre.info) at Cranfield University School of Management for permission to use some of the lessons we have used in partnership with them.

Finally, thanks to our fellow cofounder James MacKinnon and the entire Fifty Lessons team for the tremendous amount of time, effort, and steadfast support for this project.

—Adam Sodowick
   Andy Hasoon
   Directors and Cofounders
   Fifty Lessons